*Irish Sea*

*St. George's Channel*

**Trinity College**

Dundalk Bay

Dundalk

Drogheda

Dun Loaghaire

WICKLOW MTS.

Wicklow

Arklow

Cahore Point

Carnsore Point

Cavan

Mullinger

Royal Canal

Grand Canal

Dublin

Kildare

Athy

Carlow

**LEINSTER**

Enniscorthy

New Ross

Wexford

Hook Head

Longford

Tullamore

**St. Patrick Statue**

Barrow

Nore

Kilkenny

Carrick-on-Sur

Waterford

Suir

Clonmel

COMERAGH MT.

Dungarvan

Youghal Bay

**I R E L A N D**

Athlone

Lough Ree

Nenagh

Lough Derg

**Rock of Cashel**

Tipperary

GALTY MTS.

Youghal

Cobh

Castlebar

Suck

Ballinasloe

Limerick

**St. John's Castle**

Fermoy

Cork

**CONNACHT**

Claremorris

Lough Mask

Lough Corrib

Galway Bay

Ennis

Mallow

Blackwater

BOGGERAGH MT.

Old Head of Kinsale

Conn

Castlebar

Westport

Galway

**MUNSTER**

Kilrush

Lake of Killarney

Bantry

Skibbereen

**CONNEMARA**

Clifden

**Cliffs of Moher**

Aran I.

Tralee

Killarney

▲ **Carrauntuohill** 3,414'

CAHA MTS

Achill Island

Clare I.

Slyne Head

Loop Head

R. Shannon

Dingle

Dingle Bay

Valencia I.

Dunmore Head

Crow Head

Mizen Head

CAROL M. HIGHSMITH AND TED LANDPHAIR

# IRELAND

## A PHOTOGRAPHIC TOUR

CRESCENT BOOKS

NEW YORK

Photographs copyright © 1998
by Carol M. Highsmith
Text copyright © 1998
by Random House Value Publishing, Inc.
All rights reserved under International and
Pan-American Copyright Conventions.

This 1998 edition is published by Crescent Books,
a division of Random House Value Publishing, Inc.,
201 East 50th Street, New York, N.Y. 10022.

Crescent Books and colophon are trademarks of
Random House Value Publishing, Inc.

Random House
New York • Toronto • London • Sydney • Auckland
http://www.randomhouse.com/

Printed and bound in China

Library of Congress Cataloging-in-Publication
Data
Highsmith, Carol M., 1946–
Ireland : a photographic tour /
Carol M. Highsmith and Ted Landphair.
p.   cm. — (A photographic tour)
Includes index.
ISBN 0-517-18757-4 (hc: alk. paper)
1. Ireland—Pictorial works. I. Landphair,
Ted, 1942–    . II. Title. III. Series: Highsmith,
Carol M., 1946–   Photographic tour.
DA982.H54   1998                      97–17917
914.504´824—dc21                        CIP

8  7  6  5  4  3  2  1

Project Editor: Donna Lee Lurker
Production Supervisor: Michael Siebert
Designed by Robert L. Wiser, Archetype Press, Inc.,
Washington, D.C.

All photographs by Carol M. Highsmith
unless otherwise credited:
map by XNR Productions, page 5; Trinity College
Library, Dublin, page 6; Waterford Crystal
Factory, pages 8–9; Hotel Spanish Arch, Galway,
page 10; The Pighouse Folk Museum, County
Cavan, pages 11–12; Public Records Office
of Northern Ireland, page 13; Bantry House,
County Cork, page 14; Enniscoe House, Castlehill,
County Mayo, page 15; Mayo North Family
History Research Centre, pages 16, 20–21;
Blarney Woollen Mills, Blarney, County Cork,
page 17; Cobh Heritage Centre, pages 18–19

THE AUTHORS GRATEFULLY ACKNOWLEDGE
THE SERVICES, ACCOMMODATIONS,
AND SUPPORT PROVIDED BY

DAN DOOLEY RENT-A-CAR

Toll free in the United States: 1-800-331-9301

IN CONNECTION WITH THE COMPLETION
OF THIS BOOK.

THE AUTHORS ALSO WISH TO THANK THE
FOLLOWING FOR THEIR GENEROUS ASSISTANCE
AND HOSPITALITY DURING THEIR VISIT
TO IRELAND:

The Irish Tourist Board
Orla Carey, Public Relations Director, New York
Catherine McKevitt, Publicity Assistant, Dublin

The Northern Ireland Tourist Board
Rosemary Evans, Publications Manager
Maebeth Fenton, Public Relations Consultant,
U.S.A.

Kevin Beatty Limousines
Herbert Park Hotel, Dublin

Enniscoe House
Castlehill, Crossmolina, County Mayo
Susan Kellett, Proprietor

Foxmount Farm
Passage East Road, Waterford, County Waterford
Margaret Kent, Innkeeper

Herbert Park Hotel
Ballsbridge, Dublin

The Hibernian Hotel
Eastmoreland Place, Ballsbridge, Dublin

Lissadell Bed and Breakfast
Pearse Road, Sligo Town, County Sligo
Mary and Brendan Cadden, Innkeepers

The Londonderry Arms Hotel
Carnlough, County Antrim, Northern Ireland

Longfield's Hotel
Fitzwilliam Street, Dublin

Lyndale Guest House
Mullantyboyle, Glenties, County Donegal
Bob and Jean Porter, Innkeepers

Mena House Bed and Breakfast
Castlecomer Road, Kilkenny, County Kilkenny
Katherine Molloy, Innkeeper

Rochestown Park Hotel
Douglas, County Cork

Spanish Arch Hotel
Quay Street, Galway

Whaley Abbey
Ballinaclash, Rathdrum, County Wicklow
Emir Shanahan, Innkeeper

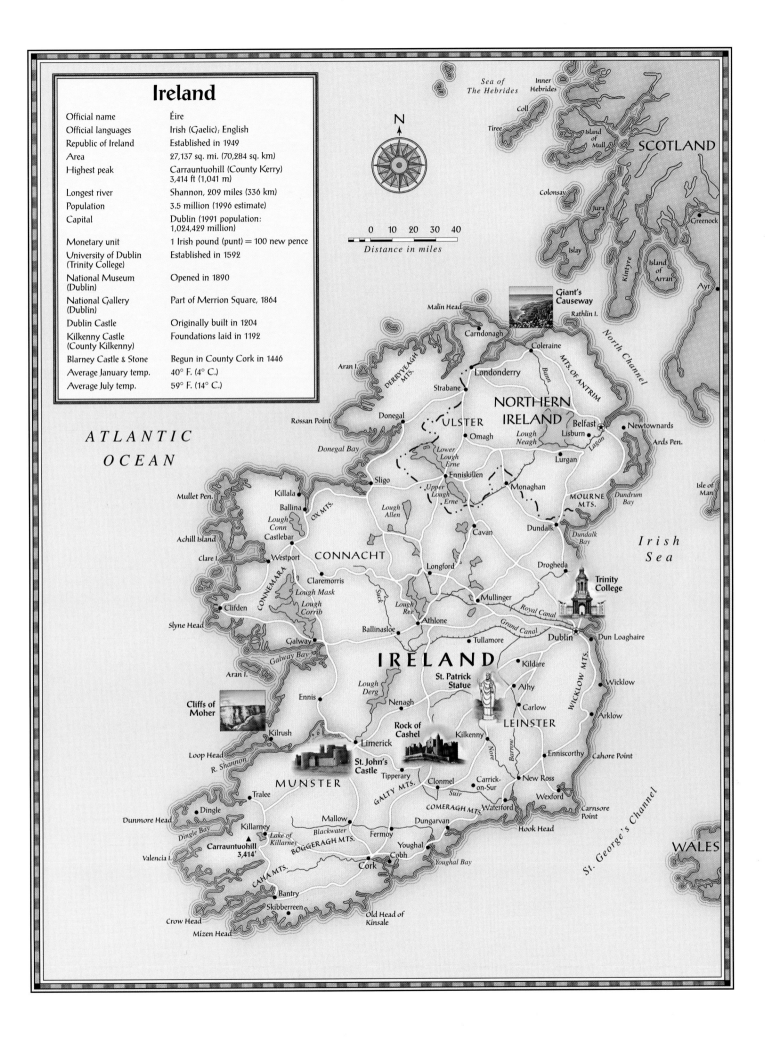

# Ireland

| | |
|---|---|
| Official name | Éire |
| Official languages | Irish (Gaelic), English |
| Republic of Ireland | Established in 1949 |
| Area | 27,137 sq. mi. (70,284 sq. km) |
| Highest peak | Carrauntuohill (County Kerry) 3,414 ft (1,041 m) |
| Longest river | Shannon, 209 miles (336 km) |
| Population | 3.5 million (1996 estimate) |
| Capital | Dublin (1991 population: 1,024,429 million) |
| Monetary unit | 1 Irish pound (punt) = 100 new pence |
| University of Dublin (Trinity College) | Established in 1592 |
| National Museum (Dublin) | Opened in 1890 |
| National Gallery (Dublin) | Part of Merrion Square, 1864 |
| Dublin Castle | Originally built in 1204 |
| Kilkenny Castle (County Kilkenny) | Foundations laid in 1192 |
| Blarney Castle & Stone | Begun in County Cork in 1446 |
| Average January temp. | 40° F. (4° C.) |
| Average July temp. | 59° F. (14° C.) |

N

0 10 20 30 40
Distance in miles

Sea of The Hebrides

Inner Hebrides

Coll

Tiree

Island of Mull

SCOTLAND

Colonsay

Jura

Greenock

Islay

Kintyre

Island of Arran

Ayr

Giant's Causeway

Malin Head

Rathlin I.

North Channel

Carndonagh

Coleraine

MTS. OF ANTRIM

Aran I.

DERRYVEAGH MTS.

Londonderry

Bann

Rossan Point

Donegal

Strabane

ULSTER

NORTHERN IRELAND

Belfast

Newtownards

ATLANTIC OCEAN

Donegal Bay

Omagh

Lough Neagh

Lisburn

Lagan

Ards Pen.

Lower Lough Erne

Enniskillen

Lurgan

Sligo

Upper Lough Erne

Monaghan

MOURNE MTS.

Dundrum Bay

Isle of Man

Killala

Lough Allen

Cavan

Dundalk

Dundalk Bay

Mullet Pen.

Ballina

OX MTS.

Irish Sea

Lough Conn

Castlebar

CONNACHT

Longford

Drogheda

Achill Island

Clare I.

Westport

Claremorris

Lough Mask

Slack

Lough Ree

Mullinger

Trinity College

CONNEMARA

Lough Corrib

Athlone

Royal Canal

Clifden

Ballinasloe

Grand Canal

Dublin

Slyne Head

Galway

Tullamore

Dun Loaghaire

IRELAND

Galway Bay

Kildare

Aran I.

Ennis

Lough Derg

St. Patrick Statue

Athy

Wicklow

Cliffs of Moher

Nenagh

Carlow

WICKLOW MTS.

Arklow

Kilrush

Rock of Cashel

Kilkenny

LEINSTER

Limerick

St. John's Castle

Tipperary

Nore

Enniscorthy

Cahore Point

Loop Head

R. Shannon

Clonmel

Carrick-on-Sur

New Ross

Barrow

MUNSTER

GALTY MTS.

Suir

Wexford

Dunmore Head

Dingle

COMERAGH MTS.

Waterford

Carnsore Point

Mallow

Dungarvan

Hook Head

Dingle Bay

Killarney

Blackwater

Fermoy

Youghal

St. George's Channel

Lake of Killarney

BOGGERAGH MTS.

Carrauntuohill 3,414'

Youghal Bay

WALES

Valencia I.

Cobh

CAHA MTS.

Cork

Bantry

Crow Head

Skibbereen

Old Head of Kinsale

Mizen Head

L OVELY. THE EXPRESSION IS THE ESSENCE OF IRELAND. You'd appreciate an early breakfast at a cozy guest house? "That'll be lovely." Paying in dollars instead of Irish pounds? "Lovely." Can stay only one night instead of two? "Lovely," again. The good-natured people of the Irish Republic and Northern Ireland are as enchanting as their land, inviting in heart and hearth, and endearingly sentimental. On first greeting a new guest from abroad, the Irish, unlike their taciturn neighbors in Northern Europe, are more than likely to offer a contagious smile and begin a pleasant conversation, or even break into song. Warmhearted hospitality is not an Irish industry, it is a part of the national character.

While there is buried in the Irish soul a quiet melancholy born of hundreds of years of invasions, famine, and the tragic and seemingly endless violence of the "Troubles," the very sensuality of the land and its people have made Ireland one of the world's most desirable tourist spots. Beyond the engaging sights and lively sounds, a visitor to Ireland will find unmatched emotional experiences. The whole of Ireland's history seems everpresent in its landscape. Its people seem to live in an almost magical and surreal communion with the past. For where else does a single crumbling ruin, standing alone in a rocky field, bear the hand of the Celts, the Vikings, the Normans, and the English? Where else are ancient Druid and Christian symbols so seamlessly juxtaposed? Where else does music so blend modern and medieval sounds? Where else can one encounter in the same realm, haunting, majestic mountains and misty glens, prehistoric tombs that predate the Egyptian pyramids, countless castles, and winding roadways bustling with the bleating of scurrying sheep?

It is little wonder that Ireland has become a popular destination for travelers of all backgrounds, and not just for those of Irish ancestry who wish to vacation in the "old country." A journey to Ireland is a pilgrimage. Whether visiting Saint Patrick's Cathedral in Dublin, the "Big Smoke" streets of Belfast, or the Shannon's languorous loughs, it is a voyage of discovery where history is not merely visited, but fully and unforgettably experienced.

The Republic of Ireland is a small country with a large capital city. Fewer than four million people live in all of the Republic, with a third of the population clustered in and around Dublin. Northern Ireland is less than half as populous. Ireland is barely larger than the U.S. state of West Virginia, but a visitor should not expect to negotiate its length and breadth with much dispatch. Even though most auto speedometers and speed-limit signs are set in miles per hour, distance signs, at the urging of the European Union, are in kilometers. Only rarely will the gauge reach sixty or seventy mph, owing to the twisting roads that usually wind past the Accident Black Spots denoting sites of fatalities and right through the heart of the busiest towns. The traveler to Ireland is certain to bring home maps, scraps of paper, and receipts and boxtops scrawled with indecipherable directions because road markers and street signs are a rarity. If you're lucky and have a sharp-eyed navigator aboard, you'll spot the name of a street posted high on a building at an intersection only to have the name change in the subsequent block.

Driving in Ireland has two advantages, however. First, because of Ireland's northerly latitude, roughly akin to that of Ontario, spring and summer days are long. The sun rises before breakfast and the sky stays luminescent well beyond a late sunset. Second, except near Dublin, there's rarely any suburban sprawl to contend with. One minute you're rounding another country bend, and the next you're in another downtown.

Kissed by the warming Gulf Stream and tender westerly winds, the island is blessed with

*The Book of Kells, one of the world's oldest and most valuable books, is an account of the New Testament's four gospels. It was lavishly illustrated and copied in Latin on calfskin by Irish monks about A.D. 800. Pictured are distinctly Irish-looking depictions of the Virgin Mother and the Christ Child.*

"soft" Irish weather as the natives call it. Cloud formations roil, but damaging storms are rare. There is no rainy season—Ireland is wet enough to stay verdant year-round—and the weather is so changeable that even meteorologists make only a halfhearted attempt to predict it. Dressing in layers is wise, for the mild air can turn frigid with a passing cloud. Not so frigid, however, to prevent palm trees from thriving on the island.

Ireland is even greener than the "forty shades of green" so often advertised. Yet it is almost treeless in stretches, and far rockier than one would imagine. It is splashed with other colors each spring, especially vivid yellows from hillsides of gorse blossoms—which the Irish call a "whin-bush"—and from fields of brilliant rape. Much of the Irish countryside is broken into little patches, which were encircled with stone fences by ancient peoples long before a tenant-farming system was imposed. The land may be green, but it is by no means loamy as most crops fare poorly, and giant combines cannot negotiate the stony soil. Instead, the Irish farm the land itself. They call it "turf," and they dry it and burn it in power plants, fireplaces, and even in the most modern of kitchen stoves. Each farm is well supplied with bricks of this peat, not stacks of firewood.

Sheep and cattle flourish in every county, but you would be hard-pressed to find a pig except in the Midlands, where they are raised in abundance in large operations behind hedgerows to supply the bacon, blood pudding, and mild sausage that are a part of the groaning board known as the "full Irish breakfast"—the other ingredients being oatmeal porridge topped with heavy granulated brown sugar and thick cream; orange juice; brown or soda bread and jam; one or two eggs; additional white toast; tomatoes and often fried potatoes; and coffee or tea.

The high hedgerows that seclude many Irish farms are not privacy measures, nor are they

*This mural by Gerald Fey depicts the Waterford crystal factory "blowing room," circa 1830. Early Waterford pieces became collectors' items when the factory closed in the 1850s. Production resumed in 1947.*

designed to heighten the discomfort of foreign drivers—used to driving on the other side of the road—whose palms are already moistened from keeping to the left along narrow country lanes. The hedges, quite simply, keep rams and ewes and lambs from wandering, and they provide cattle with a handy windbreaker on the infrequent occasions that Irish winds turn raw.

Even as Ireland grows more prosperous, with urban ghettos and rural shanties almost unknown, the Irish have seldom had the disposable income to lavish on decorative embellishments at home. The quintessential Irish thatched cottage, festooned with vivid flower boxes and curtains of delicate lace, is rare because of the costly upkeep that the reeds on the roof require. The Irish save their panache in architecture for their pubs and shops, and the occasional rowhouse door. These are dressed in the brightest and glossiest of reds, blues, purples, greens, and yellows, while the typical Irish dwelling is a mundane stucco or stone.

Four thousand years before Christ, Ireland's first inhabitants arrived from Scotland, it is hypothesized, by a long-since-vanished land bridge. Farmers and herdsmen, they built monumental rock "portal tombs," including a vast, circular chamber at Newgrange on a ridge north of the River Boyne. To this day, at dawn—precisely at the moment of the winter solstice—a beam of sunlight shines through an opening in the roof, travels along a sixty-two-foot passage, and strikes a recess in the burial chamber. Little wonder there's a ten-year waiting list to see this event in late December each year.

The Irish were descendants of the people whom the Romans called Gauls and barbarians after they knocked on the doors of Rome itself. Fierce Celtic chieftains ruled Ireland for centuries, and the people mastered both agriculture and the art of metalworking between skirmishes with one another. Surprisingly, following the arrival of a little known missionary named Patrick in A.D. 432, the Celts quickly embraced Christianity. According to legend, Patrick was first brought to the island by pirates a year earlier but escaped and fled to France, where he converted to Christianity and then returned to Ireland to preach the gospel. So powerful was Patrick's aura, it is said, that he drove every snake into the sea, and there is not a serpent to be found in the wild on the island to this day.

The Christianized Celts not only produced a civilized culture on the Irish island, they also spread Christianity and literacy across England to much of northern Europe. The Celts continued as many as one hundred chiefdoms in Ireland under four traditional kingdoms that became the island's traditional provinces: Munster, to the southwest; Leinster, around Dublin and south and westward; Connaught, in the west and northwest; and Ulster to the north. The island was mapped and divided into its present thirty-two counties in 1585.

Over time the Celtic language developed into what we today call Gaelic, a language that has endured even after British domination drove it underground. After independence in 1921, the study of Gaelic became mandatory in southern Ireland's schools. Today, "Irish," the term now preferred, is an optional subject, but interest in the language is more passionate than ever. Immersion courses in southwest Ireland and the Aran Islands are oversubscribed, road signs and tourist literature are officially bilingual, and Irish is robustly spoken on the docks and in the pubs of Ireland's western reaches. Many young authors and poets are writing in Irish, finding it a richer language than English.

The island was an easy target for invasion, though curiously, not by the Romans, who wrote of Ireland from their homes in France but never ventured to the Irish isle. (A pity, say Irish wags, for had the Romans come, perhaps the roads would have been better.) In the late eighth century the Vikings began invading Ireland periodically. The Norsemen pillaged monasteries

*Tourists visiting Galway in the late nineteenth century rode in considerably less comfort than they do today. Most arrived by rail from Dublin before setting off to see the sights.*

and towns and founded the walled cities of Dublin, Waterford, and Limerick, and eventually departed or intermarried with the native Celts. The Anglo-Normans, however, fresh from the Norman conquest of England in 1066, arrived in Ireland to stay. Normans such as Richard de Clare—known as "Strongbow"—were invited newcomers, but most others advanced armies across the countryside and King Henry II of England eventually proclaimed himself overlord of Ireland as well. The Normans built great castles in Trim, Limerick, Carrickfergus, and elsewhere, but resurgent Irish clans drove them out of many other parts of the island.

In the seventeenth century, England broke with the Catholic Church and began a two-hundred-year Protestant Ascendancy that spilled into Ireland. James I began a plantation system in the northern reaches of Ireland, and by 1703, Protestant Englishmen owned more than 75 percent of Irish land. Subjugation of the Irish, however, was achieved only after fierce battles and memorable sieges, notably by Oliver Cromwell, Lord Protector of England, whose armies ruthlessly enforced Protestant settlement. In 1782, Ireland was granted its own parliament, which met for eighteen years. But any notion of Irish sovereignty within the British Empire died with the Act of Union that sent Ireland's representatives back to London in 1800.

In the nineteenth century, Ireland was overcrowded with a population of more than eight million people, most of them barely subsisting tenant farmers and their large families packed around the fringes of baronial estates. At the time, milk and the hearty potato, nutritious and easy to grow in small plots, were so reliable a food staple that the average Irish workingman consumed fourteen pounds of the tubers a day. Cash crops—oats, corn, and wheat—and the occasional pig would be sold to pay the landlord's rent. On special occasions, such as the end of a harvest, the peasants would throw a "stampy party." "Stampies" were patties made from grated raw potatoes, flour, and seasoning. Poor as they were, and so dependent upon a single food, the Irish were Europe's healthiest people—taller, heftier, less sickly, and longer-living than

*A family in County Roscommon pose before their modest cottage in 1902. Because wood was scarce, thatched roofs were prepared from reeds harvested from either fresh- or saltwater estuaries.*

*"Turf," or peat, was harvested from the bogs and carried home for burning in fireplaces and stoves. Piles of dried peat bricks can still be seen outside dwellings throughout Ireland.*

any peasants in Great Britain or the Continent. Potato-crop failures, and even short-lived famine, were not unknown. They were considered bad fortune or a curse, to be endured until the next year's crop. So when a blight carried in the air by spores from France blackened virtually all of Ireland's potato leaves and putrefied the tubers in the crop of 1845, the Irish endured, supported by charities and the belief that next year's crop would be auspicious.

When that crop and those of the following year, and the next and next, turned up black and rotted as well, misery turned to catastrophe. Workhouses could not hold the destitute. Merciless landlords destroyed tenants' homes for nonpayment of rent. Cholera and starvation took whole families. Funerals were so frequent that carpenters constructed reusable coffins with trap doors. With help from relatives abroad or from landlords glad to be rid of the rabble, the fortunate found passage to Canada, Australia, or the United States aboard crowded steamers, never to see their homeland again. Because of the passengers' weakened state and the presence of cholera, these vessels were called "coffin ships." Knowing the penalty, many Irishmen deliberately slaughtered their landlords' cattle, or worse, so they would be "transported" to prison in Tasmania, which they believed to be a better fate. The pattern of emigration from Ireland in search of a better life was thus entrenched. Only recently has the situation abated with the return to Ireland of many of its "best and brightest," and by the rich exchange of ideas, resources, and visitations among those of Irish descent around the world.

The Great Famine was but one of many cataclysms in Ireland's tumultuous modern history. Battles for Catholic emancipation and Irish home rule, inspired by Daniel O'Connell, Charles Parnell, and others in the nineteenth century, culminated with the seizure of Dublin's General Post Office by twenty-five hundred Irish insurgents on Easter Sunday, 1916. The insurrection was quelled five days later, but the fourteen leaders executed for treason became martyrs in the drive for independence. Ireland was granted limited home rule immediately following the armistice ending World War I, and after more bloody conflicts between British troops and Irish republicans, the Anglo-Irish Treaty proclaimed the bulk of the island as the

"Irish Free State" in 1921. Six largely Protestant Northern Ireland counties, however, voted to remain in the United Kingdom.

In 1937 a new constitution in southern Ireland changed the nation's name to Éire. In 1949 it changed to the Republic of Ireland when the nation severed all ties to the British Commonwealth. Today, members of the house of representatives, the lawmaking body of the *Dáil*—the Irish Parliament—are elected proportionately from around the country. The majority party or coalition selects a prime minister, whose title in Irish—*taoiseach*—translates as "chief." Members of the smaller senate are appointed by the prime minister and other authorities. Ireland's chief executive, the president, is elected separately. In 1973 the Irish Republic joined the European Economic Community (now the European Union), opening it to expanded trade and developmental grants that have helped modernize industry, highways, and airports. In Northern Ireland, while the great smokestack industries of Belfast suffered in the wake of global modernization, European Union and British funds have produced some of Europe's most efficient cities and sleekest roads.

It was in Northern Ireland that Saint Patrick founded his church at Armagh in County Down, and the city is still thought of as the spiritual capital of the entire island. In plantation towns like Londonderry, built around central squares that the locals call "diamonds," the Anglo-Irish built bustling shops and stately Victorian homes inside one of the most complete ancient city walls still standing. The town and county, still stubbornly called just "Derry" in southern maps and conversation, have borne the brunt of sectarian strife.

Northern Ireland's volcanic County Antrim coastline is a treasure-trove of beach and golfing resorts like Portrush and Portstewart Strand, deep forests laced with waterfalls, marble-arch caves, some of Ireland's best-preserved castles, and bizarre natural wonders. The most baffling is the Giant's Causeway, a procession of basalt columns along the seashore, created by massive volcanic eruptions sixty-one million years ago. So say geologists but not Irish storytellers. According to them, a giant, Fianna clan leader Finn MacCool, laid the thousands of columns from the Irish cliffs across to Scotland—where similar formations can be found today—as a pathway for his lady love.

Single-malt, single-grain Irish whiskey—a word that comes from a Gaelic word that means "water of life"—was introduced in the little Northern Ireland town of Bushmills in the fifteenth century and licensed there in 1608. Refugee French Huguenot weavers introduced fine linenmaking to the area a few years later, though today mostly abandoned linen mills mark the "Linen Triangle" that once stretched from Belfast to Armagh to Dungannon. World-famous decorative Belleek Pottery is still produced in that little border town, however. The ill-fated *Titanic* was built in Belfast as were other ships, and the city also produced millions of feet of rope and uncounted millions of cigarettes. Despite its ties to the Industrial Revolution, Belfast, with its fine Queen's University and innumerable bookstores and libraries, became known as the "Athens of the North."

Ulster, as the province is still known despite the loss of counties Donegal, Monaghan, and Cavan to the new Irish Republic, is also home to nine wild river glens and the Glenariff Forest that William Makepeace Thackeray, the famed English novelist, called "Switzerland in miniature."

*Victorian ladies pose atop a dolmen—an ancient burial marker of intricately balanced stone slabs—inside a cromlech near Castlewellan, County Down. A cromlech is a circular series of monoliths.*

*The Rose Drawing
Room fills one corner
of County Cork's
Bantry House, where
French and Flemish
tapestries grace the
opulent mansion.
A current view of the
room is on Page 74.*

Ten U.S. presidents, beginning with Andrew Jackson, and other American notables like F. Scott Fitzgerald and Sam Houston, traced their lineage to the Ulster counties.

In the Irish Republic counties of Donegal, Leitrim, and Sligo to the west of Northern Ireland, the influences of wild scenery, Celtic mythology, and passionate poetry converge. Donegal—Gaelic for "fort of the foreigners"—was named for the Viking invaders who resided there for a time. It is Ireland's most remote county, furthest from Dublin in mindset as well as miles, though many Dubliners—and a fair number of Ulstermen as well—have built vacation cottages in the county. Road signs are exclusively in Irish here, and the independent ways of the county's mountaineers and fishing families are legend. Simple soda bread called "sohdy," now a staple of Irish breakfasts on the fanciest of guest-house tables, was first baked here. So remote is Donegal that the early Irish called it "the edge of the known world." The valleys, aflame with purplish heather and wild sage, have the look of the Scottish highlands. Donegal beaches are golden and often deserted. Though Ireland never had the resources to become a great seafaring nation, you'd never know it to watch thousands of haddock and plaice, brill and monkfish being sucked at one time out of giant trawlers and unloaded into lines of waiting trucks at the Donegal fishing port of Killybegs.

Sligo Town is a modest port at the mouth of the River Garavogue, but the county that surrounds it is better known—and aggressively promoted—as "Yeats Country." The renowned poet William Butler Yeats was born and reared here, and often returned with his brother, painter Jack Yeats, and wrote that "Sligo has always been my home." W. B. Yeats is buried in the graveyard of the Protestant Church of Ireland church in Drumcliff, where his father had been rector. The gravestone bears the epitaph, "Cast a cold Eye/ on Life on Death./ Horsemen pass by!" Visitors to County Sligo are sure to be directed to everything else Yeatsian, including Rohan Gillespie's

*Lough Conn fishing has been a passion at County Mayo's Enniscoe House— a thirty-seven-pound pike caught in 1911 is displayed to this day—but bicycling ranks a close second.*

angular bronze statue of the poet laureate downtown. Not just poetry is venerated here, for Sligo is also a lively visual-arts center full of studios and craft shops as well. Rising high above the Sligo plain is Benbulben Mountain, a noted visage of Celtic lore. The county's Lough Gill, as large as Sligo Harbor, is one of Ireland's favored boating and trout-fishing retreats.

Tiny County Leitrim is drumlin country. A drumlin is a small, oval hill formed by glacial drift, and the Leitrim landscape is ringed with them. The Irish call Leitrim the "Cinderella county," and its historic poverty and privation during the Great Famine, and waves of emigration that seemed to empty the county in the middle twentieth century, surely bore some wicked stepmother's trademark. No glass slipper yet fully fits the beautiful county, but towns like Carrick-on-Shannon and Ballinmore are again alive with commerce and nightlife.

Ocean mist, and the mists of legend, hang over Ireland's western counties: Mayo, Galway, and Roscommon. Normans fortified themselves against the Gaelic clans here, and Galway City today—burgeoning though it is as a university town, high-tech center, and tourist destination—retains the labyrinthine grid of a walled medieval town. Spanish traders once unloaded their goods at the Spanish Arch outside the city walls, and part of the Spanish Armada sailed close enough to Ireland to wreck on the rocks of County Clare south of here. Galway's Quay Street competes for the title as Ireland's most colorful shopping venue. More than half of the residents of the surrounding county, and nearly all the one thousand or so residents of the three Aran Islands offshore, claim Irish as their first language.

Contributors to a book on Irish counties called Galway "a republic within a republic; a principality of all the Irish pleasures; a dominion of dreams; a myth that is a rock-tipped reality; a myth upon which real purple heather grows; against whose shoreline the long Atlantic waves murmur mysteries." Heavy "hookers"—tanned-sail fishing boats made from heavy timber—

*The town well in Crossmolina, County Mayo, was many people's source of water. Rural neighbors often helped each other with chores like washing, peat-gathering, sheep-shearing, and fencebuilding.*

still ply the waters of Galway Bay, and a potent moonshine called *poitín* is still brewed in Connemara's mountain hollows. On the three Arans, most of the colorful native dressers and mule-cart drivers have bowed to progress—donning baseball caps and driving minivans—but the chance to see the islands' astounding seven-thousand-mile web of stone fences and to ride a bicycle in relative serenity still prompts day-trippers to pack the passenger ferries to the Arans from Galway, Doolin, and Spiddal.

County Roscommon is a place of great castles, loughs, and the ancestral home of the O'Conor clan that produced eleven high kings of Ireland. Roscommon Town is a busy market community where "Lady Betty" once negotiated her own pardon for murdering her son by agreeing to become the town hangwoman. Out in the countryside, in the stable yards of a great English estate at Strokestown, is the moving Famine Museum, which tells the story of not only the Great Famine—in which Strokestown Park's cruel landlord, Major Denis Mahon, was murdered by his tenants—but also of episodes of famine and starvation worldwide.

Ireland's "holy mountain," Croagh Patrick, rises above Clew Bay in County Mayo. Patrick was said to have fasted for forty days here while he prayed for the Irish. On the last Sunday of July, called "Reek Sunday," tens of thousands of pilgrims climb the mountain to hear Mass and receive Holy Communion. Over the years, their feet have worn a deep furrow along the path to the summit. Below them, a statue of Patrick looks out to sea. It was along the wild Mayo coastline that Stone Age inhabitants methodically ringed more than four square miles of open land in a stone wall—since largely submerged in bogs—within which they grew wheat and raised cattle.

Thanks to their majestic beauty, and to the explosive growth of Shannon's airport (where Irish coffee was invented to serve "cold and dispirited" transatlantic passengers during the propeller days of the 1940s) as an international gateway, nearby southwestern counties—Clare, Cork, Kerry, Limerick, and Tipperary—are often Ireland's first-visited and most popular destinations. The River Shannon, Ireland's longest, flows past medieval towns, lush grasslands, and a number of Celtic fortifications and widens into five great loughs along its route from the northwest highlands to the sea near Limerick. Two prodigious eighteenth-century manmade waterways from Dublin—the Grand and Royal canals—reached the Shannon and thus the agricultural riches of the Midlands and the West of Ireland.

The great Southwest is at once wild and cultivated. In northwest County Clare one encounters the eerie Burren. The name derives from the Irish word for "rocky land," but it might as well translate as "the barren." Here, rainwater has gouged deep crevices and caves into pillows of limestone, and an array of alpine flora splashes the austere landscape with surprising color. Told that the Burren was a "savage land, yielding neither water enough to drown a man, nor a tree to hang him, nor soil enough to bury him," Oliver Cromwell and his armies gave the place wide sway. Nearby is arguably Ireland's most photographed site, the dramatic Cliffs of Moher, a five-mile-long sheer rockface rising more than seven hundred feet out of the sea. At sunset, the cliffs shimmer in hues reminiscent of America's Grand Canyon, as waves crash below.

The Southwest is also castle country. There are two—King John's and Bunratty—in Limerick alone, and whole blocks of houses made from red bricks once used as ballast in ships on the great Atlantic trade routes. Rising out of the Tipperary plain is the majestic Rock of Cashel, which is a promontory, Gothic cathedral, and medieval castle all in one. Saint Patrick visited Cashel in A.D. 450, and a carving on the face of an old Irish cross—now preserved inside the Rock's museum with a copy outside—is said to be that of the island's patron saint. There are additional castles and priories to be explored at Athassel, Cahir, Thurles, and Ormand as well. In Cahir, too, is a classic example of a *cottage orné*—an enchanting, restored, thatched-roof country "Swiss" cottage. It is in little Adare, south of Limerick, though, where thatched roofs parade, one beside another, along the village's main thoroughfare. Today these brightly colored cottages are shops or rental units within sight of stately Adare Manor, a grand estate that is now a luxury hotel and golfing resort.

Cork, Ireland's largest county, includes the bulk of the "Golden Vale"—one of the tightest concentrations of dairyland in Western Europe—and the Irish Republic's second-most-populous city. Though Cork City boasts the largest natural harbor in the world, it is a drowsy port, noted as much for its secondhand shops and bohemian clubs as for its trade with the nearby European Continent. Cork has long been a center of republicanism; British "Black and Tan" troops torched the town center during the Irish Revolution, and Michael Collins, commander of the new Provisional Government's army following independence, was killed from ambush in West Cork, near Macroom, a year later.

Also in County Cork is Blarney Castle, where thousands of visitors climb its more than 120 twisting steps to kiss the Blarney Stone each year to gain, so it is said, the gift of eloquence. The legend derives from the exasperation of Britain's Queen Elizabeth I, whose demands upon Cormac MacCarthy—Lord Blarney—were met with so many oratorical obfuscations that she is said to have exclaimed, "Blarney, Blarney! What he says, he does not mean."

*Blarney Woollen Mills, seen here about 1910, are still a popular source of handwoven Irish knitwear, especially sweaters, shawls, and scarves. The outlet is a stone's throw from Blarney Castle.*

From Cork's ocean harbor at Cobh (which the Irish pronounce "Cobe") sailed the ill-fated *Titanic* and *Lusitania,* as well as two million Irish emigrants, fleeing the Great Famine. That exodus and more that followed, and the deportation of more than forty thousand convicts to Australian penal colonies, are marked at an exhibition center in Cobh's old Queenstown railway station and in a poignant statue of the woman and her younger brothers who would become the first persons admitted to New York's Ellis Island immigrant center. An old Irish ballad recalls the pain of leaving home:

> I am bidding farewell to the land of my youth and the home that I love so well.
> And the mountains so grand in my own native land, I am bidding them all farewell.
> With an aching heart, I'll bid them adieu, for tomorrow I'll sail far away,
> O'er the raging foam for to seek a home on the shores of A-mer-I-kay.

Those who left Cobh for an uncertain future, who were neither prisoners nor paying customers, or whose way was not being sponsored by a kindly relative abroad, could work as hands aboard the "coffin ships" in return for passage. But they had to make the journey twice before their debt was considered paid.

Some of Ireland's greatest scenic vistas are in County Kerry, which is home to the lovely Lakes of Killarney and the menacing Ring of Kerry. The latter is a 112-mile circular route along the high mountain ridges of the Iveragh Peninsula—with an optional white-knuckle ride over the spine of the peninsula along an even higher "scenic route." The Ring's views of mountain and coastal scenery and of sheep wandering free on the road are memorable, but truth be told, even more spectacular vistas—minus the lumbering tour buses—await visitors on the alpine road from Kenmare to Bantry. And Kerry's Dingle Peninsula, jutting west into the Atlantic Ocean, offers its own "ring" of spectacular views. The Dingle road dips down to delightful beaches and veers past pagan and Christian relics, and there's another optional heart-stopping alternate route available over Connor Pass.

*Many of the millions of emigrants who departed from Cobh bade their homeland farewell in prayer at massive Saint Colman's Cathedral. Its forty-seven-bell carillon is the largest in Ireland.*

Ireland's prosperous southeastern counties—Waterford, Wexford, Carlow, Wicklow, Kildare, and Kilkenny—are the center of great houses, castles, and orderly farmsteads, as well as some of its oldest towns, owing to their proximity to Britain. The Vikings, and later, the Anglo-Normans, were quick to invade and erect castles here, and the English influence led to the building of magnificent Palladian mansions throughout the region. Among them is Powerscourt at the foot of Wicklow's Great Sugar Loaf Mountain, just twelve miles from the center of Dublin. Powerscourt's ornamental gardens, dolphin pond, Italianate stairway, and even a pet cemetery are lavish reminders of an opulent era. Further inland, Kilkenny Castle dominates a medieval city of Tudor houses, clock towers, inns, cathedrals, and castles.

In Waterford, a modern European port is wrapped around an ancient Viking town. Craftsmanship is prized at the Waterford Crystal factory, founded in 1783, and at a heritage center that recounts the city's long history of industrialization. Neighboring County Wexford at times seems closer to Great Britain and France (via ferries to South Wales, Le Havre, and Cherbourg) than to the rest of Ireland, and this

*Eight hundred survivors from the two thousand passengers aboard the* Lusitania, *sunk by German U-boats in 1915, gather in Queenstown—which later reverted to its Irish name, Cobh, following independence.*

seabound county has been a center of English speakers for centuries. Wexford is known for its "mummers"—bands of strolling singers—and for Ireland's only indigenous Christmas carol, *The Wexford Carol.* Wexford is home to great wildfowl reserves and the John F. Kennedy Park and Arboretum—several acres of cultivated woodlands and gardens opened in 1968 in memory of the late American president. There's another famous refuge well suited to contemplation in the Irish Southeast: expansive Japanese gardens created between 1906 and 1910 at Tully in County Kildare. But Kildare is best-known as Ireland's premier horse country. It claims three of the nation's leading flat tracks, a favorite steeplechase course, and dozens of stud farms. Tiny, rural County Carlow stands just "beyond the Pale"—the area around Dublin that traditionally marked the limits of English influence. In this frontier, Irish chieftains were permitted to retain their tribal lands so long as they agreed to rear their offspring inside the Pale.

The eight counties of the Irish Midlands—Meath, Westmeath, Louth, Monaghan, Cavan, Longford, Offaly, and Laois—are off tourists' beaten paths, in part because the high-speed "M" dual carriageways radiating out from Dublin carry visitors so quickly through them. Yet this vast area of lakes, bogs, and forests is Ireland's spiritual center, the cradle of much of the island's civilization, and the home of myriad sacred and symbolic sites. Ireland's priceless decorated medieval manuscript, the *Book of Kells,* now preserved at Dublin's Trinity College, was kept at a monastery at Kells in County Meath, where it may have been written in the ninth century. There's an Iron Age fort at the Hill of Tara, and a mysterious, circular Celtic passage grave at Newgrange, both also in County Meath.

Great castles and cathedrals—Athlone in Westmeath, Drumiane in Cavan, Clonmacnoise and Birr in Offaly, Tullynally in Westmeath, Dunmaise in Laois—abound in the Midlands, free of any tourist crush. There are modest soybean and barley farms here—fertilized by liquid "slurry"—and, of course, millions of sheep and their attendant motley sheepdogs. Each sheep is marked with two colors of dye called a "riddle." Rain does not affect it, but lukewarm sudsy water at fleecing time removes the riddle dye. The Midlands are the ideal place to inspect Ireland's vast boglands that cover more than fifteen percent of the island's terrain. By hand or with huge peat-cutting combines, the Irish harvest and then dry turf from the bogs that nature has laid over thousands of years. Acids in the boglands preserve organic material so perfectly that farmers have found sticks of butter preserved intact in the places they were stored generations ago.

"Dublin's Fair City," the Irish Republic's cosmopolitan capital, marked one thousand years as a settlement in 1988. Only after the Vikings arrived from Denmark in the ninth century, stayed and intermarried with the local Celts, and established a trading post at the confluence of the rivers Liffey and Poddle in the area of a black pool (*dubh linn* in Irish), did much of a city take hold. Dublin first prospered under the English Protestants in the eighteenth century, when the Irish capital was for a time the second-largest city, behind London, in the British Empire. Rows of great Georgian mansions were built north of the Liffey, and students converged on the city from across the vast empire. But wealth later moved south again to Ballsbridge, Merrion Square, and Saint Stephen's Green. Dublin was savaged during the War of Independence, when the Custom House, Four Courts, and several shops along O'Connell Street were burned.

But the arts continued to thrive. It was in Dublin that George Frideric Handel first performed his *Messiah* on the organ. Brendan Behan read his melancholy poetry at the Abbey Theatre. Oscar Wilde lived in town. So did James Joyce in more than fifteen locations, including the old "Martello Tower" that the British had built as a lookout site in anticipation of a Napoleonic invasion. And Jonathan Swift was college dean in town. The return of a parliament to Dublin, Ireland's acceptance into the European Union, and Dublin's growing reputation as an inter-

*Lisaniska Primary School students parade during a school play in County Mayo in 1915. Soon afterward, the gunfire around them turned real during Ireland's War of Independence.*

national music, club, and restaurant scene have spurred expansion of the city, especially southeast toward the San Francisco-like hills of the Dalkey headland.

To this day, there's not a skyscraper to be found in Dublin or all of Ireland. The city's tallest building reaches just thirteen stories. Local legend has it that the populace took one look at it and determined never to make the same mistake again. But Dublin's historical attractions are so numerous that they fill entire guidebooks. They include Trinity College, founded by Queen Elizabeth I in 1592. Officially called the University of Dublin, the beautiful old college is best known for its ornate "Long Room," where a collection of illustrated medieval manuscripts, including the *Book of Kells,* is displayed. Devotees of great architecture are drawn to Dublin's classic Georgian Custom House, to Christ Church and Saint Patrick cathedrals, and to the stately Bank of Ireland building that served as chambers for the first Irish parliament. More modestly, other vestiges of Dublin's age of Georgian elegance—terraced houses, crowned doorways, and wrought-iron balconies—have become attractions unto themselves. So have the crowded, cobbled streets of the Temple Bar "arts zone"—Dublin's Greenwich Village. Rock stars are opening restaurants here and building houses on the heights south of town. Movie crews seem as commonplace as double-decker buses. Old "Dirty Dublin" has become "Party Dublin," rocking till all hours to the point that visitors are tempted to inquire, "Is everyone here under thirty?"

Until recently, Irish food had been a gustatory delight only for those who savored rich dairy products, lavish pastries, heavy meats, and "pub grub" like stout and fish and chips (fried potatoes). There's no more ubiquitous symbol in all of Ireland—not even the shamrock—than the giant plastic ice-cream cone that beckons passersby to the creamy confections dispensed by nearly every little grocer in the land. But increasingly, top chefs are migrating to Ireland's hot cities, offering creative—and slimming—salads and soups, and light gourmet dishes featuring the island's incomparable fresh fish.

Comely, tidy Ireland is at once almost unchanged yet radically different from the Ireland of forty years ago. There are more red cars and many fewer horsecarts. More "take-away" restaurants and big airports and television channels. More bed-and-breakfast inns and guest houses and comfy hostels. A quantum increase of internationally acclaimed Irish singers and artists and poets. There's still a slight out-migration, as many young people still leave in search of better career opportunities. But more and more of them are returning, and both the Irish Republic and Northern Ireland are building lively paths of exchange—through travel, trade, and on the Internet—with Irish expatriates around the world. It's part of the Irish way of tying the present with the shadows of the past, of giving everyday life a historical context. Even the Great Famine, an event that the Irish long looked upon with shame for their imprudent dependence upon a single crop and for their helplessness at confronting their plight, has become a lively topic of Irish scholarship.

Ireland's timeless antiquities, its wild cliffs and glens and barrens, its inviting homes and pubs, and its warm and sentimental people together deliver unforgettable emotional experiences to be savored and shared. Green, gregarious Ireland kindles visitors' senses, refreshes the mind, stirs the soul. They may go home, but Ireland will never leave them.

*With far less upkeep and, often, many of the same comforts, bicycles and motorbikes were a speedy alternative to the ubiquitous Irish horsecart. Motorcycle rallies are still an Irish passion.*

*OVERLEAF: O'Connell Bridge over the River Liffey is named for "The Liberator," Daniel O'Connell. In the 1920s, the brilliant County Clare lawyer fought for Catholic emancipation and an end to the Act of Union that had centralized government in London. Just across the bridge is a statue of O'Connell.*

The Bank of Ireland operates out of the Dublin building (left) that housed the Irish Parliament under eighteenth-century British rule. Tellers' cages have replaced the old House of Commons, but the House of Lords' ornate tapestries, chandelier, and oak woodwork can still be observed during banking hours. The center of British power, Dublin Castle (above), dates to 1204. Once a jail and later the home of the British viceroy to Ireland, the palace is now used for city offices and ceremonies. The Custom House (overleaf), topped by the figure of Hope, was gutted by fire during the 1921 battle for independence. It has been extensively renovated.

Kilmainham Gaol (opposite) was in use throughout the nineteenth century and into the twentieth, when it housed many political prisoners charged with fomenting revolution.

Fourteen leaders of the 1916 Easter Rising were executed by firing squad in the prison. The last prisoner held there was Eamon de Valera, who would become prime minister and later president of

Ireland. The prison is now a museum, tracing the long Irish struggle for independence. The 1802 Four Courts building (above) housed the Common Pleas, Exchequer, King's

Bench, and Chancery courts. In 1922, after an "Irish Free State" won its independence, dissidents opposing the treaty held out in the building but were bombarded into surrender by forces of the

new Irish government. The building was severely damaged, and precious historical documents housed in the adjacent Public Records Documents were destroyed by fire, and a civil war began.

Glossy doorways, such as this entryway on Baggot Street (above), are a Dublin tradition dating to the eighteenth-century age of elegance. Fanlights, bright paint hues, and eclectic door knockers add distinctiveness to the city's terraced townhouses. A ninety-eight-foot campanile, or bell tower (right), rises from the center of the Trinity College green. But the school's most famous land-mark is inside. The Old Library's 210-foot Long Room (opposite) houses more than two hundred thousand ancient texts and the oldest known harp in Ireland. The college was founded by Elizabeth I in 1592 in order "to civilise Ireland with both learning and the Protestant religion."

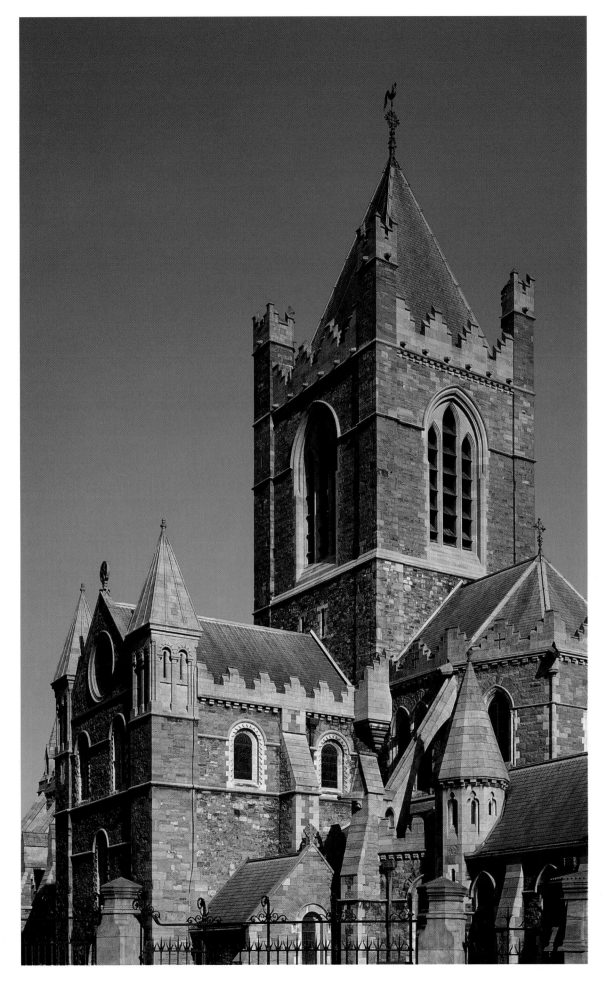

The twelfth-century Saint Patrick's Cathedral in Dublin (opposite) is Ireland's largest church. Patrick is said to have baptized converts at a well on the site in A.D. 450. But the church, in which banners and hatchments of the Knights of Saint Patrick line the magnificent choir, is now the national cathedral of the Protestant Church of Ireland. Another Church of Ireland cathedral, Christ Church (left)—the seat of the Anglican Bishop of Dublin—was commissioned in 1172 by "Strongbow," the Anglo-Norman conqueror of Dublin. The 1864 National Gallery of Ireland (overleaf) features outstanding Irish art and examples of other schools and periods of European painting. One of its leading benefactors, Irish playwright George Bernard Shaw, left one-third of his estate to the gallery.

Dublin is a city rife with statues. Sculptor Jeanne Rynhart's figure of Molly Malone (above)—legendary purveyor of cockles and mussels—at the top of the vibrant Grafton Street shopping district, was completed in 1988. The work is saucily known locally as "The Tart with a Cart." The James Joyce statue (right) on the Earl Street pedestrian mall was created by sculptor Marjorie Fitzgibbon, cast at the Dublin Art Foundry, and unveiled in 1990. John Coll's likeness of Irish writer Patrick Kavanagh (opposite) sits along Ireland's Grand Canal in Dublin. Kavanagh is quoted on an inscription: "Leafy-with-love banks and the green waters/ the canal pouring redemption over me."

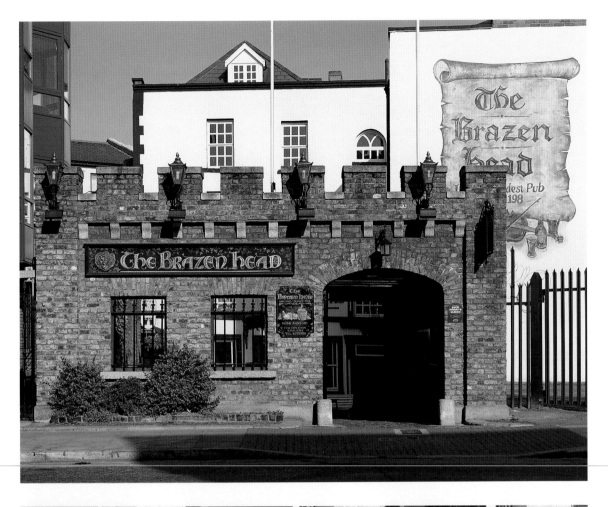

The Ha'penny pedestrian bridge across the Liffey (opposite), built by an English ironworker in 1816, got its name from the half-cent toll that was charged to cross it until 1919. The heavily traveled bridge connects Liffey Street with Dublin's teeming Temple Bar arts and music district. The Brazen Head Pub (top left) on Bridge Street is Ireland's oldest pub, dating to 1198. John Mulligan's establishment (bottom left) on Poulbeg Street was long a newspaper workers' hangout in the years that the Irish Times offices were located next door. Mulligan's was a "whiskey bonder," meaning it bought strongly fermented whiskey in bulk, diluted it following a certain formula, and resold it. There are almost one thousand pubs in Dublin alone. Throughout Ireland, their colorful façades and homey atmosphere attract customers.

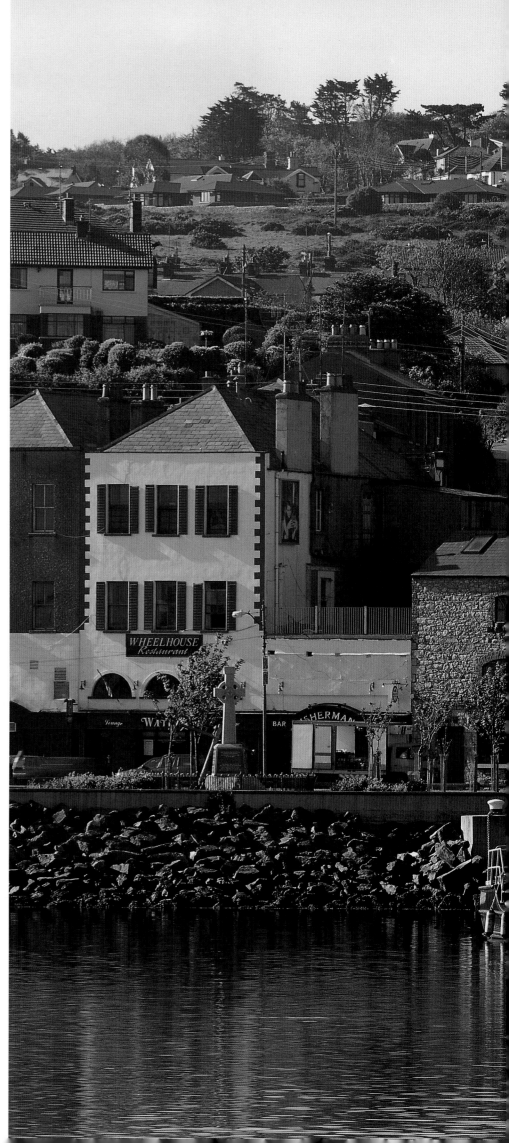

The little port of
Howth (right) in
Dublin County is
lined with seafood
dealers (above), com-
panies that make
deep-sea nets, and
other maritime opera-
tions. On weekends,
Dubliners greet
offloading trawlers,
looking for bargains
on freshly caught fish.
To the south of the
city, hillside neighbor-
hoods on Damon
Hill and Dalkey
(overleaf), overlooking
Killiney Bay, have
become some of

Ireland's most exclu-
sive neighborhoods.
Rock stars like u-2's
Bono, as well as other
notables in the worlds
of entertainment and
politics, have built fine
homes in these hills.
Peeking from behind
the hill at Sandycove
in the distance is the
Martello Tower in
which James Joyce
once lived and wrote.
The tower was built
during Napoleonic
times as an outpost
against possible
French invaders.
None arrived.

The imposing Saint Lawrence Gate— a barbican or dual circular towers linked by double arches— is all that remains of the medieval wall that protected the County Louth town of Drogheda (left) at the mouth of the River Boyne. In 1649, Oliver Cromwell's men massacred three thousand defenders of Drogheda. In 1690 at the decisive Battle of the Boyne, the forces of deposed Catholic King James II of England were defeated by an international army of Protestants. Protestants then controlled much of Ireland for more than two centuries. Saint Patrick's Cathedral (opposite) is a landmark in Dundalk—the last large town between Dublin and the Northern Ireland border. The County Louth town was the northernmost point of "the Pale," the area ruled by Anglo-Normans during the Middle Ages.

45

Newgrange mega-
lithic tomb, an
underrecognized
wonder of the ancient
world in County
Meath (opposite),
was built hundreds
of years before the
pyramids of Egypt
were constructed.
Pagans are thought
to have mined granite
in the Mourne Moun-
tains of County Down
and quartz in County
Wicklow, hundreds
of miles distant, then
carried the stone to
Newgrange by water.
Once a year for a few
minutes at the winter
solstice, light shines
through an opening
of the "passage grave"
(top right), down a
narrow corridor, to
the former threshold
of the dead in a
central chamber.
In the first through
fourth centuries A.D.,
the Hill of Tara
(bottom right), in
County Meath's
verdant Boyne Valley,
was the seat of Druid
high kings who con-
trolled the entire
north half of Ireland.

Navan (opposite) is a pleasant County Meath market and factory town. The last owner of Athlumney Castle in Navan, a devout Catholic named Sir Lancelot Dowdall, burned the tower house to the ground rather than surrender it to the forces of King William of Orange after the Battle of the Boyne. Just below the nearby Hill of Tara, the highest point in Leinster Province, Des Maguire and friend (left) tend to the garden of the Seamróg Bed-and-Breakfast Inn. Nearby are several fields of vivid yellow rape (above), an herb of the mustard family whose seeds are cultivated for oil and bird food. The crop, which vividly breaks the countryside's green monotony each Spring, was introduced to Ireland from the European continent relatively recently.

Trim in County Meath was another boundary town of the Pale, radiating outward from Dublin. The ruins of Trim Castle (above) cover two and one-half acres along the River Boyne. Built in the late twelfth century, Ireland's largest Anglo-Norman castle was a setting for Mel Gibson's movie Braveheart—about a Scottish chieftain. For the movie, set designers added faux walls and towers to the castle's remains. Afterward, the town began a massive excavation and restoration of the castle. Just across the river (right) are Saint Mary's Abbey—now a school—and the remnants of the "Yellow Steeple," where Jonathan Swift, author of Gulliver's Travels, once lived. The Viceroy of Ireland, John Talbot, turned part of the abbey into a manor house in the 1400s.

The twin towers of the Cathedral of Christ the King (left) dominate the skyline of Mullingar in County Westmeath. The cathedral, built in 1939—modern by Irish standards—is filled with mosaics by Russian-born artist Boris Anrep and features an ecclesiastical museum. Included is a model of the cathedral made from almost sixty-nine thousand matchsticks.

The River Shannon, longest in the Ireland and the British Isles, runs through the little town of Lanesborough, dividing County Longford and County Roscommon. Enthusiastic sport divers as well as fishers dip into the Shannon from boats (above), barges, and the shoreline. In nearby Lanesborough is one of Ireland's many giant peat-burning power plants.

*Birr Castle (opposite) in County Offaly was built by Sir Lawrence Parsons in the 1620s on lands once controlled by the "hospitable, fierce, yellowhaired" O'Carroll clan. Members of the family, who were titled by the British Crown as the Earls of Rosse, filled their demense—the land surrounding a mansion or castle— with a moat, still deep but now overgrown; a spectacular, one-hundred-acre ornamental garden; and a building housing the "Leviathan of Birr," a telescope that stood as the world's largest from the 1840s to 1917. Astronomers from around the globe traversed the peat bogs of the Irish Midlands to gaze through Birr's giant scope. Today the castle's formal gardens feature flowering magnolias, a prolific wisteria (right), and box hedges reputed to be the tallest in the world.*

Near the County Laois town of Mountrath stands Ballyfin House, regarded as one of the finest eighteenth-century manor houses in Ireland. The house, which is now part of a school run by the Patrician Order, includes the elaborate "Gold Room," a dining area that suggests Versailles, and features an extensive conservatory (opposite) attributed to Richard Turner, designer of the Palm House in London. The French influence is not entirely capricious. Isolated County Laois—pronounced "Leash"—was a favored haven for French Huguenot refugees, many of them well-bred military officers who established several small communities among the bogs and forests. Overlooking the estate's small artificial lake, dug by the first owner, Sir Charles Henry Coote, the Patrician fathers have erected an impressive statue of Saint Patrick (left).

The Japanese Gardens (above) at Tully, County Kildare, were laid out in the first decade of the twentieth century, during an "Orientalism" craze among wealthy landowners. Now a popular retreat not far from Dublin, the gardens share the grounds with the National Stud, a state-run breeding farm for thoroughbred horses that is also a Kildare tourism highlight. Ireland's heaviest dolmen is the Browne's Hill Portal Tomb (right), thought to date to 4000 B.C., near Tullow in County Carlow. The capstone is estimated to weigh one hundred tons. Powerscourt Estate (overleaf) in Enniskerry, County Wicklow, features aristocratic walled, Italian, and Japanese gardens that, together, are ranked among the most magnificent gardens in the Western World.

The fishing village of Kilmore Quay (opposite) sits at the tip of Forlorn Point in County Wexford. Lobster boats ply Ballyteige Bay from this popular resort, which features several whitewashed, thatched-roof guest houses and rental cottages and a lively seafood festival during the second week of July. The county's Tower of Hook (left) is the oldest lighthouse in Ireland and Great Britain. It was built atop a massive medieval tower as a landmark and lookout post early in the thirteenth century to guide ships past the Hook Peninsula's treacherous rocks. Monks from nearby Churchtown served as the tower's first custodians. A lamp was not added until 1677. Shipwrecks were so numerous in the area that their spoils were an important local source of income and provisions.

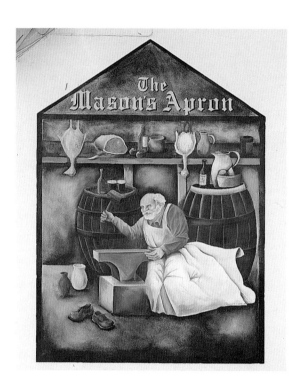

The town of Kilkenny, in the county of the same name, is Ireland's "medieval capital." Visitors can inspect cathedrals, a 1582 alms house, several grand homes, and an abbey that dates to 1225. But the centerpiece is Kilkenny Castle, bought from its twelfth-century builders by the Butlers, an Anglo-Norman clan whose descendants lived in the castle until 1935. In its fabulous Long Gallery (right) hang great tapestries and portraits of the Butler family. Aside from clever beer-sponsored signs, outdoor murals are not abundant in Ireland. But there's a masterful one (above) touting a pub in Urlingsford, County Kilkenny, that manages to work in two hearty pints of stout.

Waterford Castle (left), on an island in the River Suir, is now a guest house, meeting site, and "sport and leisure" country club. The castle is filled with Elizabethan oak paneling, great stone walls and fireplaces, sixteenth-century plaster ceilings, and antique furnishings. It was built, then enlarged over several centuries, by the Fitzgeralds, whose patriarch landed in Waterford during the 1160 Norman invasion of Ireland. Like all engravers at the Waterford Crystal factory, Thomas Hogan (above) has memorized the design of a creation before he begins his delicate work. A more remote County Waterford attraction is Ardmore Tower (overleaf), one of the best-preserved examples of the defensive "round towers" that once abounded in Ireland. It rises next to the ruins of the twelfth-century Saint Declan's Cathedral.

Sculptor Jeanne Rynhart of Bantry created the Emigrant Statue (above) on the wharf in Cobh, County Cork, from which millions of poor Irish departed their homeland. Today, more than sixty million people worldwide claim Irish ancestry. The statue depicts Annie Moore and her brothers Anthony and Philip. Annie would be the first person admitted to the immigration center on Ellis Island in New York on January 1, 1892. Cork (right), Ireland's second-largest city, was a primary exporter of Irish dairy products. In town is a memorial center to Irish Free State leader Michael Collins, who was killed in an ambush during the Irish Civil War that followed independence.

Antique stores and secondhand shops like Fitzpatrick's (opposite) entice bargain-hunters in Cork. Blarney Castle (left) in County Cork, once the home of the MacCarthy Clan that controlled Munster Province, is best known today for a stone high in its parapet, the kissing of which is reputed to bring a visitor the gift of blarney (exaggerated eloquence)— or as another legend has it, the privilege of telling lies for seven years. The smooch is accomplished on one's back, following a discomfiting stretch backward over a sheer precipice. Jerry Brady (above), an advertising executive from Annapolis, Maryland—and a descendant of the Bradys of County Cavan—accomplished the deed, to the bemusement of his wife, Arden. Afterward, he reported only a modest gain in eloquence.

The eighteenth-century Bantry House (right) of County Cork, one of Ireland's most magnificent manor houses, overlooks Bantry Bay and its delightfully named islands: Hog, Rabbit, Horse, Whiddy, and Lousy Castle. For five years, beginning in 1920, the house served as the local hospital after the town clinic burned during the War of Independence. In 1945, Bantry House became Ireland's first great manor to be opened to the public. It is now a bed-and-breakfast inn, where guests take tea in the Rose Drawing Room (above). To the northwest, sightseers along the imposing "Ring of Kerry" road get spectacular views of the River Kenmare (overleaf) and deep, rocky valleys.

Off a back road
on County Kerry's
Dingle Peninsula is
the dry-stone
Gallarus Oratory
(opposite). Built
around the seventh
or eighth century,
this early Christian
chapel resembles
an inverted boat.
A slight sagging has
occurred in the upper
portions of the roof.
The Dingle Peninsula,
seen from another
precipitous "ring"
road, also offers
ancient stone forts,
beehive huts, quaint
fishing harbors, and
some of Ireland's best
beaches. The trout
and salmon in County
Kerry's picturesque
Lakes of Killarney in
Killarney National
Park are legendary,
as are the vistas
of the three lakes.
"Ladies' View" of the
Upper Lake (above)
gets its name from
the delight expressed
by Queen Victoria's
ladies in waiting
when they visited
the overlook in 1861.
At one of the region's
most scenic spots
near Dinis Island,
the waters of Lough
Leane, Muckross
Lake, and the Upper
Lake converge.

Twenty Slattery's "caravans" (opposite) take tourists on a designated trail around the town of Tralee, the gateway to the Dingle Peninsula in County Kerry. Visitors may also rent an entire rig—horse and all—for a week or longer to explore the countryside on their own. Tralee is also home to the Siamsa Tire—the National Folk Theater of Ireland—whose performances depict many aspects of Irish culture. The quaint village of Adare, south of Limerick, is a place to find several of Ireland's best-conserved thatched-roof cottages (top and bottom, left). In the early nineteenth century, the third earl of Dunraven, master of the nearby Adare Manor, laid out the entire village, which has retained much of its charm. Three abbeys and a twelfth-century castle are nearby.

It took twenty years, from 1832–1851, to complete Adare Manor (left) in the village that is now the foxhunting center of Ireland. Today the mansion is a luxury hotel. Stonemason James Connolly carved into the south parapet words from Psalm 127: "Except the Lord build the house, the Labour is but lost that built it." Visitors can behold exquisite examples of Irish lace curtains (above), which are also abundantly available in craft shops in town. The twelfth-century King John's Castle (overleaf) in Limerick—rebuilt after being nearly destroyed by William of Orange's Protestant forces in the seventeenth century—rises imperiously above the mouth of the River Shannon.

Perhaps Ireland's most elegant "cottage orné"—or English cottage designed to reflect the "purity" of simple peasant life in architectural sympathy with its natural surroundings—is the Swiss Cottage (right), near Cahir in County Tipperary. Built in the early 1800s, it was patterned after similar cottages that originated in France during the time of Marie Antoinette. The building was an occasional residence and retreat of Richard Butler, Twelfth Lord Cahir. A "golden rain" tree (above) lends a resplendent touch to the graveyard of the Church of Saint Cronan in Roscrea, County Tipperary, one of Ireland's oldest towns. Nearby are remnants of several towers in what was once a walled fortress.

It's a hard hike from the parking lot up to the overlook at the Cliffs of Moher (left) in County Clare, but worth the exertion. An eccentric landlord, Cornelius O'Brien, built a lookout tower to impress visitors, but the view from its base is spectacular enough. The cliffs were formed as pounding waves ate away at the soft shale and sandstone of Hag's Head, where Liscannor Bay meets the Atlantic Ocean. A stone barrier has been erected along the treacherous path leading to the overlook to prevent foolhardy visitors from venturing too close to the edge. It's a precaution that is not always heeded. The Poulnabrone dolmen (above) is one of four in County Clare's austere Burren— a painter's paradise and one of the world's most distinctive floral barrens.

The three Aran Islands, off the coast of County Clare, have been called an "open-air museum," where the Irish language still thrives. Colorful Aran costumes no longer abound, horsecarts must share the road with motorized mini-van jitneys, and there's even a supermarket on the largest island, Inishmore. But the incredible maze of stone fences, myriad winding paths and sandy dunes, quaint currachs (canvas fishing boats coated with tar and equipped, these days, with outboard motors), and fascinating ruins like Inishmore's "Seven Sisters" (above) still draw throngs of visitors. The great mosaic of the Crucifixion in the retrochoir at Galway's Cathedral of Our Lady Assumed into Heaven and Saint Nicholas Church (opposite) was designed by Patrick Pollen and executed by Irish Mosaics of Roscommon. Nicholas is the patron saint of sailors. The Renaissance-style cathedral, dedicated in 1965, rose on the site of the old Galway jail.

Quay Street (right) is one of several narrow, colorful shopping corridors in Galway, one of Europe's fastest-growing cities. The bustling university city is the gateway to the picturesque Connemara Mountains, the Cliffs of Moher, and the desolate Burren. Thanks to its isolation in the West of Ireland, Galway maintained relative independence from British (or any other) rule. It developed a lively wine and spice trade with Spain and Portugal that outstripped even London and Bristol, and acquired a bohemian arts tradition that thrives to this day. Outside the Dew Drop Inn downtown is one of the classic droll Guinness stout signs (above) that proliferate throughout Ireland.

Club pro Tom Devereux, left, and guest Michael McAloran pause en route to the course at Ashford Castle (opposite) in Cong, County Mayo. The Gothic-style castle, rebuilt in 1870, is now a luxury hotel and a golf, hunting, shooting, and fishing center. Adjacent Lough Corrib boasts some of Europe's best salmon and trout fishing. It was in Cong that the melodramatic movie The Quiet Man, starring John Wayne and Maureen O'Hara, was filmed. Close by is the little village of The Neale, once home to John Browne, the first Englishman known to settle in Ireland. Browne's descendant, Lord Kilmaine, memorialized a nephew who had been killed in Egypt by building a pyramid (above), atop which he hoisted a weather vane—since demolished. The system of ostracizing overbearing landlords—later termed "boycotting"— originated in The Neale after a Captain Boycott attempted to raise local rents.

Enniscoe guest house is a Georgian mansion overlooking Lough Conn in County Mayo. Those who declared the manor—with its tightly spiraling staircase leading to a skylighted hallway (left), twenty-foot ceilings, sumptuous rooms, trophy-walled entrance hall, open fire and four-poster beds—a Heritage House of Ireland called Enniscoe "the last great house of North Mayo." Around the grounds are stables, a walled organic market garden, verdant pastureland, and a civilized forest (opposite). Not far away, on the River Addergoole where it empties into Lough Conn, old and young fishermen (above) cast for salmon. The first woman president of Ireland, Mary Robinson, grew up in Ballina in County Mayo. The area was so poor and remote, it was left to be conquered last by most of Ireland's invaders.

Sheep are plentiful in County Roscommon (above)—home of the great Connaught Kings—as they are just about everywhere else in Ireland. Lamb can be found on most fine menus, and Irish wool is renowned. Tolbernalt, one of Ireland's most treasured holy wells (opposite), is tucked in a clearing near the shores of Lough Gill in County Sligo. During "penal times," when Oliver Cromwell forbade Catholic worship, lookouts would keep vigil as priests said Mass in this sylvan setting. Like many Norman towns in Ireland, Sligo Town has its castle and its abbey (overleaf). The castle was destroyed in the fourteenth century, but the Dominican friary, founded in 1253 by Maurice Fitzgerald, survives. Its sculpted altar is the only remaining example in any Irish church. Sligo had the misfortune of being located on the shifting border between Connaught and Ulster provinces, and thus was subjected to frequent clan warfare.

W. B. Yeats's poetry is inscribed on the bronze statue (above) of "Yeats Country's" favorite son in Sligo Town. Ireland's best-known man of letters was educated in Dublin and London, but he wrote adoringly of his mother's family home in Sligo, where he spent many years. There's a Yeats room at the Sligo Town museum and art gallery, and the Yeats Memorial Building is the center for an annual summer-school scholarly gathering. Benbulben (opposite) rises starkly from the County Sligo plain; the mountain can be climbed, but it is a dangerous venture. There's a legend that a silver bell from the Sligo Town abbey was thrown into tranquil Lough Gill (overleaf), and only those free from sin can hear it peal. Some of Yeats's most sensuous poems described Innisfree, an island in Lough Gill, and the distant Benbulben plain.

Leitrim, one of
Ireland's loveliest and
least populated
counties, is blessed
with natural wonders:
deep woods, secluded
lakes, and magnificent
waterfalls, such as
the one at Glencar
(right). Throughout
alpine Northwest
Ireland—and in
Northern Ireland
as well—one hears
whispers about
"Little People." You
may catch a furtive
glimpse of a darting
figure among the
undergrowth, but
leprechauns are best
studied from their
likeness in a lawn or
woodland ornament
(above). Donegal
Castle (opposite)
was the property of
sixteenth-century clan
leader Hugh O'Don-
nell, who is said to
have burned it rather
than surrender it
to the English. An
Englishman rebuilt it,
and added an adjoin-
ing manor house.

Throughout the Irish Republic, which is more than 90 percent Roman Catholic, First Communion Day is a proud family and community occasion—a chance for third-grade children to receive their initial Holy Eucharist and, for the first time, confess their sins to a priest. It is also a chance for the youngsters to dress in finery and for proud parents to snap photographs. Here, three children (opposite) in the little County Donegal village of Glenties enjoy a moment after church in front of the statue of Our Lady of Lourdes at Columbus School. Such delightful scenes are repeated many hundredfold across the country. Thatched-roof houses are not a common sight in County Donegal— at least not in full size. But at the Lyndale Bed-and-Breakfast Inn outside Glenties is an artful facsimile in miniature (above), atop a carefully cultivated terraced garden.

Almost 20 percent
of Ireland was once
bogland, formed by
thousands of years
of vegetative decay.
There's an informa-
tive Peatlands Park
near Dungannon,
County Tyrone, in
Northern Ireland that
explains the process.
"Turf," as the Irish
call it, is harvested by
hand and by clatter-
ing machines such
as the one (right) in
County Donegal.
They slice long rows of
earth for drying and
forming into bricks.
The stripping is
rapidly depleting the
island's peat layer,
and an active conser-
vation movement is
working to preserve
the remaining bogs
that are home to birds
and unique flora. The
Irish also work hard
to preserve another
resource—their
valuable lambs. Bob
Porter of Glenties,
County Donegal,
sometimes must
take over feeding
chores (opposite)
when a ewe rejects
a lamb or is killed.

Saint Patrick's Purgatory (left) is a Roman Catholic pilgrimage site on an island in Lough Derg, between County Donegal and Northern Ireland. The faithful take a ferry over for one or three days of fasting, prayer and contemplation, and purging. At a folk museum called the Pighouse Collection in Cornafean, County Cavan, Mrs. Phyllis Faris has preserved relics of simple, long-ago Irish life, including decorative bread hardeners (above). They were used to cool bread and harden its crust after baking. Many of the everyday objects, from pie molds to griddles to washboards, are displayed in an actual large pighouse. Regrettably, rust from years of mist in the hills has taken a toll on some of the artifacts, adding an extra air of urgency to preserving the collection.

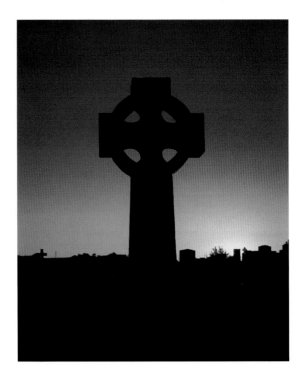

The Irish are re-
nowned for the care
with which they craft
their inspiring Celtic-
Christian memorial
crosses, such as this
example (above) from
County Monaghan in
the Midlands. Their
circular braces are dis-
tinctive, and many
Irish crosses are elabo-
rately inscribed with
intricate carvings
depicting biblical
events. Castle Coole
(right), set in vast
public parkland near
Enniskillen in County
Fermanagh, is owned
by the Northern
Ireland branch of
Britain's National
Trust. More of a
mansion than a castle,
the former home of
the earls of Belmore is
Ireland's most impres-
sive Palladian struc-
ture. Palladianism
refers to the influence
of Italian Renaissance
architect Andrea
Palladio, perhaps
the world's most-
imitated architect.

Northern Ireland is delightfully diverse. As this sheep pasture in County Tyrone (above) illustrates, it is rural, green, and serene. Many of the North's forests, canyons, and waterfalls are remote and underexplored.

Cities like Londonderry—with its medieval wall and Guildhall city hall (opposite)—come alive with entertainment and cultural opportunities each evening and weekend. During World War II,

more than twenty thousand American sailors were stationed in Derry, where the largest convoys of escorts for Allied ships crossing the Atlantic were centered. Northern Ireland's natural mysteries

such as Giant's Causeway (overleaf) rival any in Europe. The Causeway— a "remnant of [geological] chaos," English novelist William Makepeace Thackeray called it—is a mass of

tightly packed basalt columns that form stepping stones into the sea. According to legend, this was the giant Finn MacCool's pathway to the object of his ardor, a female giant on the Scottish island of Staffa.

*King James I granted the Bushmill Distillery, in the County Antrim town of Bushmills, less than a mile from the spectacular Giant's Causeway, the original license to distill "Acqua Vitae"—Irish malt whiskey—in 1608. Today the Old Bushmills Distillery (top right) is open for guided tours and a taste of its single-malt, single-grain product. Old Bushmills is a member of the Irish Distillers Group, based at the historic Jameson Heritage Center in Midleton, County Cork, in the Irish Republic. Jameson is another classic Irish whiskey. On the coast road between Carnlough and Cushendall in County Antrim is one of the Irish isle's most charming stone cottages (bottom right). The lushness of Northern Ireland glens such as this one near Craigavon in County Armagh (opposite) is almost blinding.*

Belfast's white-lime-stone City Hall (right), built in 1906, is the city's hub on Donegall Square. Its effusive architecture contrasts to the many efficient business buildings of this great shipyard center of the post-Industrial Revolution. The first meeting of the Northern Ireland Parliament was held here in 1921, before the legislature moved on. In the oak-paneled council chamber, flashing red, white, and blue lights spring to life when city council members exceed their ten-minute speaking allotment. Outside are a memorial to the victims of the 1912 S.S. Titanic disaster—the ship had been constructed in Belfast—and a rather stern statue of Queen Victoria (above).

Master Belfast architect Charles Lanyan modeled his design for the Tudor-style Queen's College building (left) on Magdalene College in Oxford. The massive building is the centerpiece of Queen's University, founded in 1849, which boasts Northern Ireland's finest schools of law, medicine, and engineering and attracts students from around the world. The campus lies south of Donegall Square, past Belfast's "Golden Mile" entertainment district. Walking from downtown to the university, one is apt to be greeted with the city's cheerful, quirky salutation: "'bout ye?"— shorthand for "How's about you?" Imposing, neoclassical Stormont (above), outside Belfast, was originally Northern Ireland's legislative building. Parliament for this portion of the United Kingdom was disbanded in 1972, so Stormont is now used for the Northern Ireland Secretary's administrative offices.

Locals in the port town of Donaghadee, County Down, call their impressive Norman castle (above) "The Moat." The building was employed as an ammunition storehouse and lookout tower during World War II. Russian czar Peter the Great stopped in Donaghadee in 1697 on his Grand Tour of Europe. The comely town is noted for its harbor walls, completed in the early nineteenth century by Sir John Rennie, who designed several of London's bridges. Excursion boats leave the harbor for the three Copeland Islands, which are uninhabited by all but sea birds. Not far from Donaghadee on the Ards Peninsula, in the crossroads community of Millisle, is the Ballycopeland Windmill (opposite), the last working windmill in Northern Ireland. Wind-power enthusiasts should also check out the 1846 Tacumshane Windmill in the Republic's County Wexford, one of the last (though inoperative) thatched windmills in Ireland.

# Index